# PEARLS IN PROVERBS

## FORWARD

*"This compilation of subjects will prove invaluable for meditation, guidance, counseling and the worship of God."*

*W.H. Borland*, Jr., Compiler

For many years, the Book of Proverbs has been of interest to me. My wife and I read one chapter a day with our children in our family devotions while they were growing up. We felt that the teachings from the Book of Proverbs would help mold the character of each one of our four children.

Early in the 1970's the first and only printing of **"PEARLS FROM PROVERBS"** came out. Mr. W.H. Borland, Jr. compiled the book and it was printed by my good friend Jim Dewberry. We immediately purchased the book and began to see what a powerful tool it could be for personal and family devotions. We purchased many copies and gave them out to our friends until the stock was depleted.

I found myself using this tool in preparation for my sermons and even taking **"PEARLS IN PROVERBS"** into the pulpit reading those verses that related to the subject on which I was preaching.

For some time now, I have felt the need to reprint the book. I have changed the format a little and have added a few extras such as *"FIVE THINGS GOD WANTS YOU TO KNOW"* under Salvation.

I pray the **PEARLS IN PROVERS** will be a blessing to you as it has been to me these many years. I would suggest you read a chapter a day from the Book of Proverbs in your Bible. You and your children need to hear the words of Proverbs often. May God richly bless you as you read and study His Word.

*Melvyn L. Brown*

Co-Compiler and Editor

**This material is used by the permission of W.H. Borland, Jr.**

# Table of Contents

| | | | |
|---|---|---|---|
| ABOMINATIONS | 1 | GIVING | 23 |
| ANGER | 3 | GOD – FEAR | 25 |
| BRAGGING | 4 | GOD – OMNIPOTENCE | 26 |
| CHASTENING | 5 | GOD – PROTECTION | 28 |
| CHILDREN'S INSTRUCTIONS | 6 | GOD - RESISTING | 30 |
| COMPANIONS - BAD | 8 | GOD – VINDICATION | 30 |
| COMPASSION | 10 | GOODNESS | 31 |
| COUNSELING | 10 | GOSSIP | 33 |
| DECEIT | 12 | GREED | 34 |
| DILIGENCE | 13 | HAPPINESS | 35 |
| DISCRETION | 14 | HATE | 36 |
| ENVY | 15 | HAUGHTINESS | 37 |
| EVIL | 16 | HEART | 37 |
| FAITH | 17 | HUMILITY | 39 |
| FEAR | 18 | INDUSTRY | 40 |
| FLATTERY | 19 | INSTRUCTION | 41 |
| FOOLS | 20 | JUDGING | 43 |

| | | | |
|---|---|---|---|
| KNOWLEDGE | 44 | PRIDE | 65 |
| LAZINESS – (SLOTH) | 45 | PRUDENCE | 67 |
| LIQUOR | 47 | REBELLION | 68 |
| LOVE | 48 | REPROOF | 68 |
| LYING | 48 | REWARDS | 71 |
| MARRIAGE | 50 | RIGHTEOUSNESS | 72 |
| MERCY | 51 | SALVATION | 75 |
| MOUTH - (the tongue) | 52 | SCORN | 78 |
| MURDER | 55 | SELF CONTROL | 79 |
| NEIGHBORS - (FRIENDS) | 55 | SELF-WILL | 80 |
| OBEDIENCE | 57 | SEXUAL IMPURITY | 81 |
| OLD AGE | 58 | SIN | 84 |
| PARENTS | 60 | SOUL WINNING | 86 |
| PEACE | 61 | STEALING | 86 |
| PERVERSENESS -(WAYWARD) | 62 | STRIFE | 87 |
| The POOR | 62 | TRUST | 88 |
| PRAYER | 64 | TRUTH | 89 |

| | |
|---|---|
| UNDERSTANDING ............... 90 | WISDOM-(Knowledge ....... 97 applied correctly) |
| WEALTH ............................... 92 | WIVES ................................ 99 |
| WICKED ................................ 94 | WOMEN .............................. 101 |

---

"All scripture is given
by inspiration of God, and is profitable

for doctrine,
(that is what is right)

for reproof,
(that is what is wrong)

for correction,
(that is how to get right)

for instruction in righteousness:
(that is how to stay right)

That the man of God may be perfect,
throughly furnished unto all good works."

2 Timothy 3:16-17

*All Scriptures are taken from the King James Bible.*

## *ABOMINATIONS*

3:32 For the froward is abomination to the LORD: but his secret is with the righteous.

6:16-19 These six things doth the LORD hate: yea, seven are an abomination unto him: A proud look, a lying tongue, and hands that shed innocent blood, An heart that deviseth wicked imaginations, feet that be swift in running to mischief, A false witness that speaketh lies, and he that soweth discord among brethren.

8:7 For my mouth shall speak truth; and wickedness is an abomination to my lips.

11:1 A false balance is abomination to the LORD: but a just weight is his delight.

11:20 They that are of a froward heart are abomination to the LORD: but such as are upright in their way are his delight.

12:22 Lying lips are abomination to the LORD: but they that deal truly are his delight.

15:8-9 The sacrifice of the wicked is an abomination to the LORD: but the prayer of the upright is his delight. The way of the wicked is an abomination unto the LORD: but he loveth him that followeth after righteousness.

15:26 The thoughts of the wicked are an abomination to the LORD: but the words of the pure are pleasant words.

16:5 Every one that is proud in heart is an abomination to the LORD: though hand join in hand, he shall not be unpunished.

17:15 He that justifieth the wicked, and he that condemneth the just, even they both are abomination to the LORD.

20:10 Divers weights, and divers measures, both of them are alike abomination to the LORD.

21:27 The sacrifice of the wicked is abomination: how much more, when he bringeth it with a wicked mind?

24:9 The thought of foolishness is sin: and the scorner is an abomination to men.

28:9 He that turneth away his ear from hearing the law, even his prayer shall be abomination.

29:27 An unjust man is an abomination to the just: and he that is upright in the way is abomination to the wicked.

# ANGER

11:4 Riches profit not in the day of wrath: but righteousness delivereth from death.

11:23 The desire of the righteous is only good: but the expectation of the wicked is wrath.

12:16 A fool's wrath is presently known: but a prudent man covereth shame.

14:17 He that is soon angry dealeth foolishly: and a man of wicked devices is hated.

14:29 He that is slow to wrath is of great understanding: but he that is hasty of spirit exalteth folly.

15:1 A soft answer turneth away wrath: but grievous words stir up anger.

15:18 A wrathful man stirreth up strife: but he that is slow to anger appeaseth strife.

16:14 The wrath of a king is as messengers of death: but a wise man will pacify it.

16:29 A violent man enticeth his neighbour, and leadeth him into the way that is not good.

16:32 He that is slow to anger is better than the mighty; and he that ruleth his spirit than he that taketh a city.

19:11 The discretion of a man deferreth his anger; and it is his glory to pass over a transgression.

19:19 A man of great wrath shall suffer punishment: for if thou deliver him, yet thou must do it again.

21:14 A gift in secret pacifieth anger: and a reward in the bosom strong wrath.

21:19 It is better to dwell in the wilderness, than with a contentious and an angry woman.

21:24 Proud and haughty scorner is his name, who dealeth in proud wrath.

22:24 Make no friendship with an angry man; and with a furious man thou shalt not go:

27:3 A stone is heavy, and the sand weighty; but a fool's wrath is heavier than them both.

27:4 Wrath is cruel, and anger is outrageous; but who is able to stand before envy?

29:8 Scornful men bring a city into a snare: but wise men turn away wrath.

29:22 An angry man stirreth up strife, and a furious man aboundeth in transgression.

## *BRAGGING*

17:19 He loveth transgression that loveth strife: and

20:6 Most men will proclaim every one his own goodness: but a faithful man who can find?

20:14 It is naught, it is naught, saith the buyer: but when he is gone his way, then he boasteth.

26:12 Seest thou a man wise in his own conceit? there is more hope of a fool than of him.

27:1 Boast not thyself of to morrow; for thou knowest not what a day may bring forth.

27:2 Let another man praise thee, and not thine own mouth; a stranger, and not thine own lips.

## *CHASTENING*

3:11-12 My son, despise not the chastening of the LORD; neither be weary of his correction: For whom the LORD loveth he correcteth; even as a father the son in whom he delighteth.

10:13 In the lips of him that hath understanding wisdom is found: but a rod is for the back of him that is void of understanding.

13:24 He that spareth his rod hateth his son: but he that loveth him chasteneth him betimes.

19:18 Chasten thy son while there is hope, and let not thy soul spare for his crying.

22:15 Foolishness is bound in the heart of a child; but the rod of correction shall drive it far from him.

23:13-14 Withhold not correction from the child: for if thou beatest him with the rod, he shall not die. Thou shalt beat him with the rod, and shalt deliver his soul from hell.

26:3 A whip for the horse, a bridle for the ass, and a rod for the fool's back.

29:15 The rod and reproof give wisdom: but a child left to himself bringeth his mother to shame.

## *CHILDREN'S INSTRUCTIONS*

1:8 My son, hear the instruction of thy father, and forsake not the law of thy mother:

4:1 Hear, ye children, the instruction of a father, and attend to know understanding.

6:20 My son, keep thy father's commandment, and forsake not the law of thy mother:

10:1 The proverbs of Solomon. A wise son maketh a glad father: but a foolish son is the heaviness of his mother.

10:5 He that gathereth in summer is a wise son: but he that sleepeth in harvest is a son that causeth shame.

13:1 A wise son heareth his father's instruction: but a scorner heareth not rebuke.

15:5 A fool despiseth his father's instruction: but he that regardeth reproof is prudent.

15:20 A wise son maketh a glad father: but a foolish man despiseth his mother.

17:25 A foolish son is a grief to his father, and bitterness to her that bare him.

19:13 A foolish son is the calamity of his father: and the contentions of a wife are a continual dropping.

19:26-27 He that wasteth his father, and chaseth away his mother, is a son that causeth shame, and bringeth reproach. Cease, my son, to hear the instruction that causeth to err from the words of knowledge.

20:20 Whoso curseth his father or his mother, his lamp shall be put out in obscure darkness.

22:15 Foolishness is bound in the heart of a child; the rod of correction shall drive it far from him.

23:22 Hearken unto thy father that begat thee, and despise not thy mother when she is old.

28:7 Whoso keepeth the law is a wise son: but he that is a companion of riotous men shameth his father.

28:24 Whoso robbeth his father or his mother, and saith, It is no transgression; the same is the companion of a destroyer.

29:3 Whoso loveth wisdom rejoiceth his father: but he that keepeth company with harlots spendeth his substance.

30:17 The eye that mocketh at his father, and despiseth to obey his mother, the ravens of the valley shall pick it out, and the young eagles shall eat it.

## *COMPAIONS - BAD*

1:10 My son, if sinners entice thee, consent thou not.

1:15 My son, walk not thou in the way with them; refrain thy foot from their path:

2:18-19 For her house inclineth unto death, and her paths unto the dead. None that go unto her return again, neither take they hold of the paths of life.

2:18-19 For her house inclineth unto death, and her paths unto the dead. None that go unto her return again, neither take they hold of the paths of life.

4:14-15 Enter not into the path of the wicked, and go not in the way of evil men. Avoid it, pass not by it, turn from it, and pass away.

12:11 He that tilleth his land shall be satisfied with bread: but he that followeth vain persons is void of understanding.

13:20 He that walketh with wise men shall be wise: but a companion of fools shall be destroyed.

14:7 Go from the presence of a foolish man, when thou perceivest not in him the lips of knowledge.

18:5 It is not good to accept the person of the wicked to overthrow the righteous in judgment.

23:6 Eat thou not the bread of him that hath an evil eye, neither desire thou his dainty meats

24:1 Be not thou envious against evil men, neither desire to be with them.

28:7 Whoso keepeth the law is a wise son: but he that is a companion of riotous men shameth his father.

28:10 Whoso causeth the righteous to go astray in an evil way, he shall fall himself into his own pit: but the upright shall have good things in possession.

29:24 Whoso is partner with a thief hateth his own soul: he heareth cursing, and bewrayeth it not.

> David said, "I am a companion of all them that fear thee, and of them that keep thy precepts." Psalm 119:63

## *COMPASSION*

3:27 Withhold not good from them to whom it is due, when it is in the power of thine hand to do it.

21:13 Whoso stoppeth his ears at the cry of the poor he also shall cry himself, but shall not be heard.

22:22 Rob not the poor, because he is poor: neither oppress the afflicted in the gate:

24:17 Rejoice not when thine enemy falleth, and let not thine heart be glad when he stumbleth:

## *COUNSELING*

1:5 A wise man will hear, and will increase learning; and a man of understanding shall attain unto wise counsels:

1:25 But ye have set at nought all my counsel, and would none of my reproof:

1:30 They would none of my counsel: they despised all my reproof.

8:14 Counsel is mine, and sound wisdom: I am understanding; I have strength.

11:14 Where no counsel is, the people fall: but in the multitude of counsellors there is safety.

12:5 The thoughts of the righteous are right: but the counsels of the wicked are deceit.

12:15 The way of a fool is right in his own eyes: but he that hearkeneth unto counsel is wise.

12:20 Deceit is in the heart of them that imagine evil: but to the counsellors of peace is joy.

13:10 Only by pride cometh contention: but with the well advised is wisdom.

15:10 Correction is grievous unto him that forsaketh the way: and he that hateth reproof shall die.

15:22 Without counsel purposes are disappointed: but in the multitude of counsellors they are established.

16:22 Understanding is a wellspring of life unto him that hath it: but the instruction of fools is folly.

19:20 Hear counsel, and receive instruction, that thou mayest be wise in thy latter end.

19:21 There are many devices in a man's heart; nevertheless the counsel of the LORD, that shall stand.

20:5 Counsel in the heart of man is like deep water; but a man of understanding will draw it out.

20:18 Every purpose is established by counsel: and with good advice make war.

22:20-21 Have not I written to thee excellent things in counsels and knowledge, That I might make thee know the certainty of the words of truth; that thou mightest answer the words of truth to them that send unto thee?

24:6 For by wise counsel thou shalt make thy war: and in multitude of counsellors there is safety.

## *DECEIT*

9:17 Stolen waters are sweet, and bread eaten in secret is pleasant.

11:18 The wicked worketh a deceitful work: but the counsels of the wicked are deceit.

12:5 The thoughts of the righteous are right: but the counsels of the wicked are deceit.

12:17 He that speaketh truth sheweth forth righteousness: but a false witness deceit.

12:20 Deceit is in the heart of them that imagine evil: but to the counsellors of peace is joy.

14:8 The wisdom of the prudent is to understand his way: but the folly of fools is deceit.

14:25 A true witness delivereth souls: but a deceitful witness speaketh lies.

20:17 Bread of deceit is sweet to a man; but afterwards his mouth shall be filled with gravel

24:28 Be not a witness against thy neighbour without cause; and deceive not with thy lips.

26:18-19 As a mad man who casteth firebrands, arrows, and death, So is the man that deceiveth his neighbour, and saith, Am not I in sport?

29:13 The poor and the deceitful man meet together: the LORD lighteneth both their eyes.

31:30 Favour is deceitful, and beauty is vain: but a woman that feareth the LORD, she shall be praised.

## *DILIGENCE*

4:23 Keep thy heart with all diligence; for out of it are the issues of life.

10:4 He becometh poor that dealeth with a slack hand: but the hand of the diligent maketh rich.

12:24 The hand of the diligent shall bear rule: but the slothful shall be under tribute.

12:27 The slothful man roasteth not that which he took in hunting: but the substance of a diligent man is precious.

13:4 The soul of the sluggard desireth, and hath nothing: but the soul of the diligent shall be made fat.

22:29 Seest thou a man diligent in his business? he shall stand before kings; he shall not stand before mean men.

27:23 Be thou diligent to know the state of thy flocks, and look well to thy herds.

## *DISCRETION*

2:11 Discretion shall prserve thee, understanding shall keep thee:

3:21 My son, let not them depart from thine eyes: keep sound wisdom and discretion:

11:22 As a jewel of gold in a swine's snout, so is a fair woman which is without discretion.

19:11 The discretion of a man deferreth his anger; and it is his glory to pass over a trans- gression.

25:11 A word fitly spoken is like apples of gold in pictures of silver.

26:17 He that passeth by, and meddleth with strife belonging not to him, is like one that taketh a dog by the ears

# ENVY

3:31 Envy thou not the oppressor and choose none of his ways.

5:15 Drink waters out of thine own cistern, and running waters out of thine own well.

14:30 A sound heart is the life of the flesh: but envy the rottenness of the bones.

23:17 Let not thine heart envy sinners: but be thou in the fear of the Lord all the day long.

24:1 Be not thou envious against evil men, neither desire to be with them.

24:19 Fret not thyself because of evil men, neither be thou envious at the wicked;

27:4 Wrath is cruel, and anger is outrageous; but who is able to stand before envy?

## *EVIL*

3:7 Be not wise in thine own eyes: fear the LORD, and depart from evil.

3:29 Devise not evil against thy neighbour, seeing he dwelleth securely by thee.

4:14 Enter not into the path of the wicked, and go not in the way of evil men.

4:27 Turn not to the right hand nor to the left: remove thy foot from evil.

8:13 The fear of the LORD is to hate evil: pride, and arrogancy, and the evil way, and the froward mouth, do I hate.

11:19 As righteousness tendeth to life: so he that pursueth evil pursueth it to his own death.

13:19 The desire accomplished is sweet to the soul: but it is abomination to fools to depart from evil

13:21 Evil pursueth sinners: but to the righteous good shall be repayed.

14:19 The evil bow before the good; and the wicked at the gates of the righteous.

14:22 Do they not err that devise evil? but mercy and truth shall be to them that devise good.

15:28 The heart of the righteous studieth to answer: but the mouth of the wicked poureth out evil things.

16:17 The highway of the upright is to depart from evil: he that keepeth his way preserveth his soul.

17:13 Whoso rewardeth evil for good, evil shall not depart from his house.

24:1 Be not thou envious against evil men, neither desire to be with them.

24:8 He that deviseth to do evil shall be called a mischievous person.

24:20 For there shall be no reward to the evil man; the candle of the wicked shall be put out.

29:6 In the transgression of an evil man there is a snare: but the righteous doth sing and rejoice.

## *FAITH*

3:6 In all thy ways acknowledge him, and he shall direct thy paths.

3:26 For the LORD shall be thy confidence, and shall keep thy foot from being taken.

8:17 I love them that love me; and those that seek me early shall find me.

8:34 Blessed is the man that heareth me, watching daily at my gates, waiting at the posts of my doors.

20:6 Most men will proclaim every one his own goodness: but a faithful man who can find?

24:10 If thou faint in the day of adversity, thy strength is small.

28:20 A faithful man shall abound with blessings: but he that maketh haste to be rich shall not be innocent.

## *FEAR*

1:26-27 I also will laugh at your calamity; I will mock when your fear cometh; When your fear cometh as desolation, and your destruction cometh as a whirlwind; when distress and anguish cometh upon you.

1:33 But whoso hearkeneth unto me shall dwell safely, and shall be quiet from fear of evil.

3:24-25 When thou liest down, thou shalt not be afraid: yea, thou shalt lie down, and thy sleep shall be sweet. Be not afraid of sudden fear, neither of the desolation of the wicked, when it cometh.

10:24 The fear of the wicked, it shall come upon him: but the desire of the righteous shall be granted.

13:13 Whoso despiseth the word shall be destroyed: but he that feareth the commandment shall be rewarded.

14:16 A wise man feareth, and departeth from evil: but the fool rageth, and is confident.

28:1 The wicked flee when no man pursueth: but the righteous are bold as a lion.

28:14 Happy is the man that feareth alway: but he that hardeneth his heart shall fall into mischief.

29:25 The fear of man bringeth a snare: but whoso putteth his trust in the LORD shall be safe.

## *FLATTERY*

7:21 With her much fair speech she caused him to yield, with the flattering of her lips she forced him.

19:6 Many will entreat the favour of the prince: and every man is a friend to him that giveth gifts. 20:19

He that goeth about as a talebearer revealeth secrets: therefore meddle not with him that flattereth with his lips.

24:24 He that saith unto the wicked, Thou art righteous; him shall the people curse, nations shall abhor him:

26:25 When he speaketh fair, believe him not: for there are seven abominations in his heart.

26:28 A lying tongue hateth those that are afflicted by it; and a flattering mouth worketh ruin.

28:23 He that rebuketh a man afterwards shall find more favour than he that flattereth with the tongue.

29:5 A man that flattereth his neighbour spreadeth a net for his feet.

## *FOOLS*

1:7 The fear of the LORD is the beginning of knowledge: but fools despise wisdom and instruction.

1:22 How long, ye simple ones, will ye love simplicity? and the scorners delight in their scorning, and fools hate knowledge?

3:35 The wise shall inherit glory: but shame shall be the promotion of fools.

9:6 Forsake the foolish, and live: and go in the way of understanding.

10:8 The wise in heart will receive commandments: but a prating fool shall fall.

10:18 He that hideth hatred with lying lips, and he that uttereth a slander, is a fool.

10:21 The lips of the righteous feed many: but fools die for want of wisdom.

11:29 He that troubleth his own house shall inherit the wind: and the fool shall be servant to the wise of heart.

12:15 The way of a fool is right in his own eyes: but he that hearkeneth unto counsel is wise.

12:23 A prudent man concealeth knowledge: but the heart of fools proclaimeth foolishness.

13:16 Every prudent man dealeth with knowledge: but a fool layeth open his folly.

13:20 He that walketh with wise men shall be wise: but a companion of fools shall be destroyed.

14:7 Go from the presence of a foolish man, when thou perceivest not in him the lips of knowledge.

14:9 Fools make a mock at sin: but among the righteous there is favour.

14:16 A wise man feareth, and departeth from evil: but the fool rageth, and is confident.

14:24 The crown of the wise is their riches: but the foolishness of fools is folly.

15:2 The tongue of the wise useth knowledge aright: but the mouth of fools poureth out foolishness.

15:5 A fool despiseth his father's instruction: but he that regardeth reproof is prudent.

15:14 The heart of him that hath understanding seeketh knowledge: but the mouth of fools feedeth on foolishness.

17:21 He that begetteth a fool doeth it to his sorrow: and the father of a fool hath no joy.

18:2 A fool hath no delight in understanding, but that his heart may discover itself.

18:6 A fool's lips enter into contention, and his mouth calleth for strokes.

18:7 A fool's mouth is his destruction, and his lips are the snare of his soul.

19:10 Delight is not seemly for a fool; much less for a servant to have rule over princes.

20:3 It is an honour for a man to cease from strife: but every fool will be meddling.

23:9 Speak not in the ears of a fool: for he will despise the wisdom of thy words.

26:4-9 Answer not a fool according to his folly, lest thou also be like unto him. Answer a fool according to his folly, lest he be wise in his own conceit. He that sendeth a message by the hand of a fool cutteth off the feet, and drinketh damage. The legs of the lame are not equal: so is a parable in the mouth of fools. As he that bindeth a stone in a sling, so is he that giveth honour to a fool. As a thorn goeth up into the hand of a drunkard, so is a parable in the mouth of fools.

28:26 He that trusteth in his own heart is a fool: but whoso walketh wisely, he shall be delivered.

29:11 A fool uttereth all his mind: but a wise man keepeth it in till afterwards.

## *GIVING*

3:9 Honour the LORD with thy substance, and with the firstfruits of all thine increase:

3:27 Withhold not good from them to whom it is due, when it is in the power of thine hand to do it.

11:25 The liberal soul shall be made fat: and he that watereth shall be watered also himself.

13:22 A good man leaveth an inheritance to his children's children: and the wealth of the sinner is laid up for the just.

17:8 A gift is as a precious stone in the eyes of him that hath it: whithersoever it turneth, it prospereth.

18:16 A man's gift maketh room for him, and bringeth him before great men.

19:6 Many will entreat the favour of the prince: and every man is a friend to him that giveth gifts.

21:13 Whoso stoppeth his ears at the cry of the poor, he also shall cry himself, but shall not be heard.

21:14 A gift in secret pacifieth anger: and a reward in the bosom strong wrath.

22:9 He that hath a bountiful eye shall be blessed; for he giveth of his bread to the poor.

25:21 If thine enemy be hungry, give him bread to eat; and if he be thirsty, give him water to drink:

28:27 He that giveth unto the poor shall not lack: but

he that hideth his eyes shall have many a curse.

## *GOD – FEAR*

1:7 The fear of the LORD is the beginning of knowledge: but fools despise wisdom and instruction.

1:29 For that they hated knowledge, and did not choose the fear of the LORD:

3:7 Be not wise in thine own eyes: fear the LORD, and depart from evil.

8:13 The fear of the LORD is to hate evil: pride, and arrogancy, and the evil way, and the froward mouth, do I hate.

9:10 The fear of the LORD is the beginning of wisdom: and the knowledge of the holy is understanding.

10:27 The fear of the LORD prolongeth days: but the years of the wicked shall be shortened.

14:2 He that walketh in his uprightness feareth the LORD: but he that is perverse in his ways despiseth him.

14:26-27 In the fear of the LORD is strong confidence: and his children shall have a place of

15:16 Better is little with the fear of the LORD than great treasure and trouble therewith.

16:6 By mercy and truth iniquity is purged: and by the fear of the LORD men depart from evil.

19:23 The fear of the LORD tendeth to life: and he that hath it shall abide satisfied; he shall not be visited with evil.

22:4 By humility and the fear of the LORD are riches, and honour, and life.

23:17 Let not thine heart envy sinners: but be thou in the fear of the LORD all the day long.

24:21 My son, fear thou the LORD and the king: and meddle not with them that are given to change:

31:30 Favour is deceitful, and beauty is vain: but a woman that feareth the LORD, she shall be praised.

## *GOD – OMNIPOTENCE*

2:8 He keepeth the paths of judgment, and preserveth the way of his saints.

3:19-20 The LORD by wisdom hath founded the earth; by understand- ing hath he established the heavens. By his knowledge the depths are broken up, and the clouds drop down the dew.

5:21 For the ways of man are before the eyes of the LORD, and he pondereth all his goings.

8:22-30 The LORD possessed me in the beginning of his way, before his works of old. I was set up from everlasting, from the beginning, or ever the earth was. When there were no depths, I was brought forth; when there were no fountains abounding with water. Before the mountains were settled, before the hills was I brought forth: While as yet he had not made the earth, nor the fields, nor the highest part of the dust of the world. When he prepared the heavens, I was there: when he set a compass upon the face of the depth: When he established the clouds above: when he strength- ened the fountains of the deep: When he gave to the sea his decree, that the waters should not pass his commandment: when he appointed the foundations of the earth: Then I was by him, as one brought up with him: and I was daily his delight, rejoicing always before him;

15:3 The eyes of the LORD are in every place, beholding the evil and the good.

16:4 The LORD hath made all things for himself: yea, even the wicked for the day of evil.

16:9 A man's heart deviseth his way: but the LORD directeth his steps.

20:12 The hearing ear, and the seeing eye, the LORD hath made even both of them.

20:24 Man's goings are of the LORD; how can a man then understand his own way?

21:1 The king's heart is in the hand of the LORD, as the rivers of water: he turneth it whithersoever he will.

22:2 The rich and poor meet together: the LORD is the maker of them all.

22:12 The eyes of the LORD preserve knowledge, and he overthroweth the words of the transgressor.

26:10 The great God that formed all things both rewardeth the fool, and rewardeth transgressors.

## *GOD - PROTECTION*

1:33 But whoso hearkeneth unto me shall dwell safely, and shall be quiet from fear of evil.

3:26 For the LORD shall be thy confidence, and shall keep thy foot from being taken.

7:2 Keep my commandments, and live; and my law as the apple of thine eye.

10:3 The LORD will not suffer the soul of the righteous to famish: but he casteth away the substance of the wicked.

10:27 The fear of the LORD prolongeth days: but the years of the wicked shall be shortened.

10:29 The way of the LORD is strength to the upright: but destruction shall be to the workers of iniquity.

10:30 The righteous shall never be removed: but the wicked shall not inhabit the earth.

11:8 The righteous is delivered out of trouble, and the wicked cometh in his stead.

12:21 There shall no evil happen to the just: but the wicked shall be filled with mischief.

14:26 In the fear of the LORD is strong confidence: and his children shall have a place of refuge.

18:10 The name of the LORD is a strong tower: the righteous runneth into it, and is safe.

20:24 Man's goings are of the LORD; how can a man then understand his own way?

21:31 The horse is prepared against the day of battle: but safety is of the LORD.

29:25 The fear of man bringeth a snare: but whoso putteth his trust in the LORD shall be safe.

30:5 Every word of God is pure: he is a shield unto them that put their trust in him.

## GOD - RESISTING

1:28 Then shall they call upon me, but I will not answer; they shall seek me early, but they shall not find me:

3:11-12 My son, despise not the chastening of the LORD; neither be weary of his correction: For whom the LORD loveth he correcteth; even as a father the son in whom he delighteth.

6:15 Therefore shall his calamity come suddenly; suddenly shall he be broken without remedy.

29:1 He, that being often reproved hardeneth his neck, shall suddenly be destroyed, and that without remedy.

## GOD - VINDICATION

1:26 I also will laugh at your calamity; I will mock when your fear cometh;

1:28 Then shall they call upon me, but I will not answer; they shall seek me early, but they shall not find me:

3:33 The curse of the LORD is in the house of the wicked: but he blesseth the habitation of the just.

6:15 Therefore shall his calamity come suddenly; suddenly shall he be broken without remedy.

11:28 He that trusteth in his riches shall fall: but the righteous shall flourish as a branch.

11:29 He that troubleth his own house shall inherit the wind: and the fool shall be servant to the wise of heart.

13:13 Whoso despiseth the word shall be destroyed: but he that feareth the commandment shall be rewarded.

15:25 The LORD will destroy the house of the proud: but he will establish the border of the widow.

21:12 The righteous man wisely considereth the house of the wicked: but God overthroweth the wicked for their wickedness.

22:23 For the LORD will plead their cause, and spoil the soul of those that spoiled them.

29:1 He, that being often reproved hardeneth his neck, shall suddenly be destroyed, and that without remedy.

## *GOODNESS*

2:21 For the upright shall dwell in the land, and the perfect shall remain in it.

11:27 He that diligently seeketh good procureth favour: but he that seeketh mischief, it shall come unto

12:2 A good man obtaineth favour of the LORD: but a man of wicked devices will he condemn.

13:21 Evil pursueth sinners: but to the righteous good shall be repayed.

13:22 A good man leaveth an inheritance to his children's children: and the wealth of the sinner is laid up for the just.

14:14 The backslider in heart shall be filled with his own ways: and a good man shall be satisfied from himself.

17:13 Whoso rewardeth evil for good, evil shall not depart from his house.

20:6 Most men will proclaim every one his own goodness: but a faithful man who can find?

22:1 A good name is rather to be chosen than great riches, and loving favour rather than silver and gold.

25:21 If thine enemy be hungry, give him bread to eat; and if he be thirsty, give him water to drink:

29:7 The righteous considereth the cause of the poor: but the wicked regardeth not to know it.

# *GOSSIP*

6:16-19 These six things doth the LORD hate: yea, seven are an abomination unto him: A proud look, a    An heart that deviseth wicked imaginations, feet that be swift in running to mischief, A false witness that speaketh lies, and he that soweth discord among brethren.

11:9 An hypocrite with his mouth destroyeth his neighbour: but through knowledge shall the just be delivered.

11:13 A talebearer revealeth secrets: but he that is of a faithful spirit concealeth the matter.

16:28 A froward man soweth strife: and a whisperer separateth chief friends.

17:9 He that covereth a transgression seeketh love; but he that repeateth a matter separateth very friends.

18:8 The words of a talebearer are as wounds, and they go down into the innermost parts of the belly.

19:2 Also, that the soul be without knowledge, it is not good; and he that hasteth with his feet sinneth.

20:19 He that goeth about as a talebearer revealeth secrets: therefore meddle not with him that flattereth with his lips.

25:9 Debate thy cause with thy neighbour himself; and discover not a secret to another.

26:20 Where no wood is, there the fire goeth out: so where there is no talebearer, the strife ceaseth.

> **SOME GOOD ADVISE:**
> "Now I beseech you, brethren, mark them which cause divisions and offences contrary to the doctrine which ye have learned; and avoid them." Romans 16:17

# GREED

1:19 So are the ways of every one that is greedy of gain; which taketh away the life of the owners thereof.

15:27 He that is greedy of gain troubleth his own house; but he that hateth gifts shall live.

22:16 He that oppresseth the poor to increase his riches, and he that giveth to the rich, shall surely come to want.

23:5 Wilt thou set thine eyes upon that which is not? for riches certainly make themselves wings; they fly away as an eagle toward heaven.

25:16 Hast thou found honey? eat so much as is sufficient for thee, lest thou be filled therewith, and vomit it.

27:20 Hell and destruction are never full; so the eyes of man are never satisfied.

28:8 He that by usury and unjust gain increaseth his substance, he shall gather it for him that will pity the poor.

28:16 The prince that wanteth understanding is also a great oppressor: but he that hateth covetousness shall prolong his days.

## *HAPPINESS*

3:13 Happy is the man that findeth wisdom, and the man that getteth understanding.

8:32 Now therefore hearken unto me, O ye children: for blessed are they that keep my ways.

8:34 Blessed is that man that heareth me, watching daily at my gates, waithing at the posts of my doors.

12:20 Deceit is in the heart of them that imagine evil: but to the counsellors of peace is joy.

14:21 He that despiseth his neighbour sinneth: but he that hath mercy on the poor, happy is he.

15:13 A merry heart maketh a cheerful countenance: but by sorrow of the heart the spirit is broken.

15:15 All the days of the afflicted are evil: but he that is of a merry heart hath a continual feast.

15:23 A man hath joy by the answer of his mouth: and a word spoken in due season, how good is it!

16:20 He that handleth a matter wisely shall find good: and whoso trusteth in the LORD, happy is he.

17:22 A merry heart doeth good like a medicine: but a broken spirit drieth the bones.

29:6 In the transgression of an evil man there is a snare: but the righteous doth sing and rejoice.

29:18 Where there is no vision, the people perish: but he that keepeth the law, happy is he.

## *HATE*

10:12 Hatred stirreth up strifes: but love covereth all sins.

10:18 He that hideth hatred with lying lips, and he that uttereth a slander, is a fool.

14:17 He that is soon angry dealeth foolishly: and a man of wicked devices is hated.

15:17 Better is a dinner of herbs where love is, than a stalled ox and hatred therewith.

## *HAUGHTINESS*

6:16-17 These six things doth the LORD hate: yea, seven are an abomination unto him: A proud look, a lying tongue, and hands that shed innocent blood,

8:13 The fear of the LORD is to hate evil: pride, and arrogancy, and the evil way, and the froward mouth, do I hate.

16:18 Pride goeth before destruction, and an haughty spirit before a fall.

18:12 Before destruction the heart of man is haughty, and before honour is humility.

## *HEART*

3:1 My son, forget not my law; but let thine heart keep my commandments:

4:23 Keep thy heart with all diligence; for out of it are the issues of life.

10:20 The tongue of the just is as choice silver: the heart of the wicked is little worth.

12:23 A prudent man concealeth knowledge: but the heart of fools proclaimeth foolishness.

14:13 Even in laughter the heart is sorrowful; and the end of that mirth is heaviness.

14:14 The backslider in heart shall be filled with his own ways: and a good man shall be satisfied from himself.

14:30 A sound heart is the life of the flesh: but envy the rottenness of the bones.

15:13-14 A merry heart maketh a cheerful countenance: but by sorrow of the heart the spirit is broken. The heart of him that hath understanding seeketh knowledge: but the mouth of fools feedeth on foolishness.

15:15 All the days of the afflicted are evil: but he that is of a merry heart hath a continual feast.

15:30 The light of the eyes rejoiceth the heart: and a good report maketh the bones fat.

15:13-14 A merry heart maketh a cheerful countenance: but by sorrow of the heart the spirit is broken. The heart of him that hath understanding seeketh knowledge: but the mouth of fools feedeth on foolishness.

15:15 All the days of the afflicted are evil: but he that is of a merry heart hath a continual feast.

15:30 The light of the eyes rejoiceth the heart: and a good report maketh the bones fat.

16:9 A man's heart deviseth his way: but the LORD directeth his steps.

19:3 The foolishness of man perverteth his wand: and his heart fretteth against the LORD.

19:21 There are many devices in a man's heart; nevertheless the counsel of the LORD, that shall stand.

20:9 Who can say, I have made my heart clean, I am pure from my sin?

21:4 An high look, and a proud heart, and the plowing of the wicked, is sin.

23:7 For as he thinketh in his heart, so is he: Eat and drink, saith he to thee; but his heart is not with thee.

23:17 Let not thine heart envy sinners: but be thou in the fear of the LORD all the day long.

28:14 Happy is the man that feareth alway: but he that hardeneth his heart shall fall into mischief.

## *HUMILITY*

6:3 Do this now, my son, and deliver thyself, when thou art come into the hand of thy friend; go, humble thyself, and make sure thy friend.

11:2 When pride cometh, then cometh shame: but with the lowly is wisdom.

15:33 The fear of the LORD is the instruction of wisdom; and before honour is humility.

16:19 Better it is to be of an humble spirit with the lowly, than to divide the spoil with the proud.

18:12 Before destruction the heart of man is haughty, and before honour is humility.

22:4 By humility and the fear of the LORD are riches, and honour, and life.

25:6-7 Put not forth thyself in the presence of the king, and stand not in the place of great men: For better it is that it be said unto thee, Come up hither; than that thou shouldest be put lower in the presence of the prince whom thine eyes have seen.

29:23 A man's pride shall bring him low: but honour shall uphold the humble in spirit.

## *INDUSTRY*

6:6-8 Go to the ant, thou sluggard; consider her ways, and be wise: Which having no guide, overseer, or ruler, Provideth her meat in the summer, and gathereth her food in the harvest.

6:9 How long wilt thou sleep, O sluggard? when wilt thou arise out of thy sleep?

12:11 He that tilleth his land shall be satisfied with bread: but he that followeth vain persons is void of understanding.

13:11 Wealth gotten by vanity shall be diminished: but he that gathereth by labour shall increase.

19:15 Slothfulness casteth into a deep sleep; and an idle soul shall suffer hunger.

22:29 Seest thou a man diligent in his business? he shall stand before kings; he shall not stand before mean men.

27:18 Whoso keepeth the fig tree shall eat the fruit thereof: so he that waiteth on his master shall be honoured.

28:19 He that tilleth his land shall have plenty of bread: but he that followeth after vain persons shall have poverty enough.

## *INSTRUCTION*

1:8 My son, hear the instruction of thy father, and forsake not the law of thy mother:

4:13 Take fast hold of instruction; let her not go: keep her; for she is thy life.

5:7 Hear me now therefore, O ye children, and depart not from the words of my mouth.

5:12 And say, How have I hated instruction, and my heart despised reproof.

8:33 Hear instruction, and be wise, and refuse it not.

9:9 Give instruction to a wise man, and he will be yet wiser: teach a just man, and he will increase in learning.

10:8 The wise in heart will receive commandments: but a prating fool shall fall.

10:17 He is in the way of life that keepeth instruction but he that refuseth reproof erreth.

12:1 Whoso loveth instruction loveth knowledge: but he that hateth reproof is brutish.

13:1 A wise son heareth his father's instruction: but a scorner heareth not rebuke.

13:18 Poverty and shame shall be to him that refuseth instruction: but he that regardeth reproof shall be honoured.

15:5 A fool despiseth his father's instruction: but he that regardeth reproof is prudent.

15:32 He that refuseth instruction despiseth his own soul: but he that heareth reproof getteth understanding.

16:22 Understanding is a wellspring of life unto him that hath it: but the instruction of fools is folly.

19:20 Hear counsel, and receive instruction, that thou mayest be wise in thy latter end.

23:12 Apply thine heart unto instruction, and thine ears to the words of knowledge

## *JUDGING*

24:23 These things also belong to the wise. It is not good to have respect of persons in judgment.

24:28 Be not a witness against thy neighbour without cause; and deceive not with thy lips.

28:21 To have respect of persons is not good: for for a piece of bread that man will transgress.

29:14 The king that faithfully judgeth the poor, his throne shall be established for ever.   :

Romans 2:1 Therefore thou art inexcusable, O man, whosoever thou art that judgest: for wherein thou judgest another, thou condemnest thyself; for thou that judgest doest the same things.

Romans 14:4 Who art thou that judgest another man's servant? to his own master he standeth or falleth. Yea, he shall be holden up: for God is able to make him stand.

## *KNOWLEDGE*

1:7 The fear of the LORD is the beginning of knowledge: but fools despise wisdom and instruction.

1:29 For that they hated knowledge, and did not choose the fear of the LORD:

11:9 An hypocrite with his mouth destroyeth his neighbour: but through knowledge shall the just be delivered.

12:1 Whoso loveth instruction loveth knowledge: but he that hateth reproof is brutish.

13:16 Every prudent man dealeth with knowledge: but a fool layeth open his folly.

14:6 A scorner seeketh wisdom, and findeth it not: but knowledge is easy unto him that understandeth.

15:2 The tongue of the wise useth knowledge aright: but the mouth of fools poureth out foolishness.

15:14 The heart of him that hath understanding seeketh knowledge: but the mouth of fools feedeth on foolishness.

17:27 He that hath knowledge spareth his words: and a man of understanding is of an excellent spirit.

19:2 Also, that the soul be without knowledge, it is not good; and he that hasteth with his feet sinneth.

20:15 There is gold, and a multitude of rubies: but the lips of knowledge are a precious jewel.

21:11 When the scorner is punished, the simple is made wise: and when the wise is instructed, he receiveth knowledge.

24:5 A wise man is strong; yea, a man of knowledge increaseth strength.

## *LAZINESS* – (SLOTH)

6:6 Go to the ant, thou sluggard; consider her ways, and be wise:

6:9 How long wilt thou sleep, O sluggard? when wilt thou arise out of thy sleep?

10:4-5 He becometh poor that dealeth with a slack hand: but the hand of the diligent maketh rich. He that gathereth in summer is a wise son: but he that sleepeth in harvest is a son that causeth shame.

12:24 The hand of the diligent shall bear rule: but the slothful shall be under tribute.

12:27 The slothful man roasteth not that which he took in hunting: but the substance of a diligent man is precious.

13:4 The soul of the sluggard desireth, and hath nothing: but the soul of the diligent shall be made fat.

18:9 He also that is slothful in his work is brother to him that is a great waster.

19:15 Slothfulness casteth into a deep sleep; and an idle soul shall suffer hunger.

19:24 A slothful man hideth his hand in his bosom, and will not so much as bring it to his mouth again.

20:4 The sluggard will not plow by reason of the cold; therefore shall he beg in harvest, and have nothing.

20:13 Love not sleep, lest thou come to poverty; open thine eyes, and thou shalt be satisfied with bread.

21:25 The desire of the slothful killeth him; for his hands refuse to labour.

24:30-31 I went by the field of the slothful, and by the vineyard of the man void of understanding; And, lo, it was all grown over with thorns, and nettles had covered the face thereof, and the stone wall thereof was broken down.

26:14-16 As the door turneth upon his hinges, so doth the slothful upon his bed. The slothful hideth his hand in his bosom; it grieveth him to bring it again to his mouth. The sluggard is wiser in his own conceit than seven men that can render a reason.

## *LIQUOR*

20:1 Wine is a mocker, strong drink is raging: and whosoever is deceived thereby is not wise.

21:17 He that loveth pleasure shall be a poor man: he that loveth wine and oil shall not be rich.

23:20-21 Be not among wine- bibbers; among riotous eaters of flesh: For the drunkard and the glutton shall come to poverty: and drowsiness shall clothe a man with rags.

23:29-36 Who hath woe? who hath sorrow? who hath contentions? who hath babbling? who hath wounds without cause? who hath redness of eyes? They that tarry long at the wine; they that go to seek mixed wine. Look not thou upon the wine when it is red, when it giveth his colour in the cup, when it moveth itself aright. At the last it biteth like a serpent, and stingeth like an adder. Thine eyes shall behold strange women, and thine heart shall utter perverse things. Yea, thou shalt be as he that lieth down in the midst of the sea, or as he that lieth upon the top of a mast. They have stricken me, shalt thou say, and I was not sick; they have beaten me, and I felt it not: when shall I awake? I will seek it yet again.

## *LOVE*

8:17 I love them that love me; and those that seek me early shall find me.

8:21 That I may cause those that love me to inherit substance; and I will fill their treasures.

9:8 Reprove not a scorner, lest he hate thee: rebuke a wise man, and he will love thee.

10:12 Hatred stirreth up strifes: but love covereth all sins.

15:17 Better is a dinner of herbs where love is, than a stalled ox and hatred therewith.

17:9 He that covereth a trans- gression seeketh love; but he that repeateth a matter separateth very friends.

## *LYING*

6:16, 17, 19 These six things doth the LORD hate: yea, seven are an abomination unto him: A proud look, a lying tongue, and hands that shed innocent blood, A false witness that speaketh lies, and he that soweth discord among brethren.

10:18 He that hideth hatred with lying lips, and he that uttereth a slander, is a fool.

12:17 He that speaketh truth sheweth forth righteousness: but a false witness deceit.

12:19 The lip of truth shall be established for ever: but a lying tongue is but for a moment.

12:22 Lying lips are abomination to the LORD: but they that deal truly are his delight.

13:5 A righteous man hateth lying: but a wicked man is loathsome, and cometh to shame.

14:5 A faithful witness will not lie: but a false witness will utter lies.

14:25 A true witness delivereth souls: but a deceitful witness speaketh lies.

17:4 A wicked doer giveth heed to false lips; and a liar giveth ear to a naughty tongue.

19:5 A false witness shall not be unpunished, and he that speaketh lies shall not escape.

19:9 A false witness shall not be unpunished, and he that speaketh lies shall perish.

21:6 The getting of treasures by a lying tongue is a vanity tossed to and fro of them that seek death.

21:28 A false witness shall perish: but the man that heareth speaketh constantly.

24:28 Be not a witness against thy neighbour without cause; and deceive not with thy lips.

25:18 A man that beareth false witness against his

## *MARRIAGE*

5:18-19 Let thy fountain be blessed: and rejoice with the wife of thy youth. Let her be as the loving hind and pleasant roe; let her breasts satisfy thee at all times; and be thou ravished always with her love.

6:32 But whoso committeth adultery with a woman lacketh understanding: he that doeth it destroyeth his own soul.

12:4 A virtuous woman is a crown to her husband: but she that maketh ashamed is as rottenness in his bones.

14:1 Every wise woman buildeth her house: but the foolish plucketh it down with her hands.

18:22 Whoso findeth a wife findeth a good thing, and obtaineth favour of the LORD.

19:13-14 A foolish son is the calamity of his father: and the contentions of a wife are a continual dropping. House and riches are the inheritance of fathers: and a prudent wife is from the LORD.

21:19 It is better to dwell in the wilderness, than with a contentious and angry woman.

24:3 Through wisdom is an house builded; and by understanding it is established:

25:24 It is better to dwell in the corner of the housetop, than with a brawling woman and in a wide house.

## **MERCY** (Mercy means, God holds back what we deserves)

3:3 Let not mercy and truth forsake thee: bind them about thy neck; write them upon the table of thine heart:

11:17 The merciful man doeth good to his own soul: but he that is cruel troubleth his own flesh.

14:21-22 He that despiseth his neighbour sinneth: but he that hath mercy on the poor, happy is he. Do they not err that devise evil? but mercy and truth shall be to them that devise good.

16:6 By mercy and truth iniquity is purged: and by the fear of the LORD men depart from evil.

19:17 He that hath pity upon the poor lendeth unto the LORD; and that which he hath given will he pay him again.

21:21 He that followeth after righteousness and mercy findeth life, righteousness, and honour.

28:13 He that covereth his sins shall not prosper: but whoso confesseth and forsaketh them shall have mercy.

## *MOUTH* - (TONGUE)

4:24 Put away from thee a froward mouth, and perverse lips put far from thee.

6:2 Thou art snared with the words of thy mouth, thou art taken with the words of thy mouth.

6:12 A naughty person, a wicked man, walketh with a froward mouth.

8:7 For my mouth shall speak truth; and wickedness is an abomination to my lips.

8:13 The fear of the LORD is to hate evil: pride, and arrogancy, and the evil way, and the froward mouth, do I hate.

10:6 Blessings are upon the head of the just: but violence covereth the mouth of the wicked.

10:11 The mouth of a righteous man is a well of life: but violence covereth the mouth of the wicked.

10:14 Wise men lay up knowledge: but the mouth of the foolish is near destruction.

10:19 In the multitude of words there wanteth not sin: but he that refraineth his lips is wise.

10:21 The lips of the righteous feed many: but fools die for want of wisdom.

10:31-32 The mouth of the just bringeth forth wisdom: but the froward tongue shall be cut out. The lips of the righteous know what is acceptable: but the mouth of the wicked speaketh frowardness.

11:9 An hypocrite with his mouth destroyeth his neighbour: but through knowledge shall the just be delivered.

12:18 There is that speaketh like the piercings of a sword: but the tongue of the wise is health.

13:3 He that keepeth his mouth keepeth his life: but he that openeth wide his lips shall have destruction.

14:3 In the mouth of the foolish is a rod of pride: but the lips of the wise shall preserve them.

15:2 The tongue of the wise useth knowledge aright: but the mouth of fools poureth out foolishness.

15:4 A wholesome tongue is a tree of life: but perverseness therein is a breach in the spirit.

15:23 A man hath joy by the answer of his mouth: and a word spoken in due season, how good is it!

15:28 The heart of the righteous studieth to answer: but the mouth of the wicked poureth out evil things.

16:23 The heart of the wise teacheth his mouth, and addeth learning to his lips.

17:28 Even a fool, when he holdeth his peace, is counted wise: and he that shutteth his lips is esteemed a man of understanding.

18:7 A fool's mouth is his destruction, and his lips are the snare of his soul.

18:21 Death and life are in the power of the tongue: and they that love it shall eat the fruit thereof.

19:28 An ungodly witness scorneth judgment: and the mouth of the wicked devoureth iniquity.

20:19 He that goeth about as a talebearer revealeth secrets: therefore meddle not with him that flattereth with his lips.

29:11 A fool uttereth all his mind: but a wise man keepeth it in till afterwards.

29:20 Seest thou a man that is hasty in his words? there is more hope of a fool than of him.

## *MURDER*

1:19 So are the ways of every one that is greedy of gain; which taketh away the life of the owners thereof.

6:16-17 These six things doth the Lord hate: yea, seven are an abomination unto him: A proud look, a lying tongue, and hands that shed innocent blood.

28:17 A man that doeth violence to the blood of any person shall flee to the pit; let no man stay him.

29:10 The bloodthirsty hate the upright: but the just seek his soul.

## *NEIGHBORS* - (FRIENDS)

3:27 Withhold not good from them to whom it is due, when it is in the power of thine hand to do it.

3:28-30 Say not unto thy neighbour, Go, and come again, and to morrow I will give; when thou hast it by thee. Devise not evil against thy neighbour, seeing he dwelleth securely by thee.

Strive not with a man without cause, if he have done thee no harm.

6:3 Do this now, my son, and deliver thyself, when thou art come into the hand of thy friend; go, humble thyself, and make sure thy friend.

11:9 An hypocrite with his mouth destroyeth his neighbour: but through knowledge shall the just be delivered.

11:12 He that is void of wisdom despiseth his neighbour: but a man of understanding holdeth his peace.

14:21 He that despiseth his neighbour sinneth: but he that hath mercy on the poor, happy is he.

17:17 A friend loveth at all times, and a brother is born for adversity.

18:19 A brother offended is harder to be won than a strong city: and their contentions are like the bars of a castle.

18:24 A man that hath friends must shew himself friendly: and there is a friend that sticketh closer than a brother.

21:10 The soul of the wicked desireth evil: his neighbour findeth no favour in his eyes.

22:24 Make no friendship with an angry man; and with a furious man thou shalt not go:

24:28 Be not a witness against thy neighbour without cause; and deceive not with thy lips.

25:9 Debate thy cause with thy neighbour himself; and discover not a secret to another:

25:17-18 Withdraw thy foot from thy neighbour's house; lest he be weary of thee, and so hate thee. A man that beareth false witness against his neighbour is a maul, and a sword, and a sharp arrow.

21:10 The soul of the wicked desireth evil: his neighbour findeth no favour in his eyes.

29:5 A man that flattereth his neighbour spreadeth a net for his feet.

## *OBEDIENCE*

1:33 But whoso hearkeneth unto me shall dwell safely, and shall be quiet from fear of evil.

4:4 He taught me also, and said unto me, Let thine heart retain my words: keep my commandments, and live.

5:12-13 And say, How have I hated instruction, and my heart despised reproof; And have not obeyed the voice of my teachers, nor inclined mine ear to them that instructed me!

7:1 My son, keep my words, and lay up my commandments with thee.

7:2 Keep my commandments, and live; and my law as the apple of thine eye.

16:7 When a man's ways please the LORD, he maketh even his enemies to be at peace with him.

19:16 He that keepeth the commandment keepeth his own soul; but he that despiseth his ways shall die.

27:18 Whoso keepeth the fig tree shall eat the fruit thereof: so he that waiteth on his master shall be honoured.

28:7 Whoso keepeth the law is a wise son: but he that is a companion of riotous men shameth his father.

29:18 Where there is no vision, the people perish: but he that keepeth the law, happy is he.

## *OLD AGE*

3:1-2 My son, forget not my law; but let thine heart keep my commandments: For length of days, and long life, and peace, shall they add to thee.

4:10 Hear, O my son, and receive my sayings; and the years of thy life shall be many.

10:27 The fear of the LORD prolongeth days: but the years of the wicked shall be shortened.

16:31 The hoary head is a crown of glory, if it be found in the way of righteousness.

17:6 Children's children are the crown of old men; and the glory of children are their fathers.

20:29 The glory of young men is their strength: and the beauty of old men is the grey head.

22:6 Train up a child in the way he should go: and when he is old, he will not depart from it.

28:16 The prince that wanteth understanding is also a great oppressor: but he that hateth covetousness shall prolong his days.

> "*The righteous shall flourish like the palm tree: he shall grow like a cedar in Lebanon. Those that be planted in the house of the LORD shall flourish in the courts of our God. They* (The righteous) *shall still bring forth fruit in old age; they shall be fat and flourishing; To show that the LORD is upright: he is my rock, and there is no unrighteousness in him.*" Psalms 92:12-15

## *PARENTS*

7:21 He that begetteth a fool doeth it to his sorrow: and the father of a fool hath no joy.

13:24 He that spareth his rod hateth his son: but he that loveth him chasteneth him betimes.

17:21 He that begetteth a fool doeth it to his sorrow: and the father of a fool hath no joy.

19:13 A foolish son is the calamity of his father: and the contentions of a wife are a continual dropping.

19:18 Chasten thy son while there is hope, and let not thy soul spare for his crying.

22:6 Train up a child in the way he should go: and when he is old, he will not depart from it.

22:15 Foolishness is bound in the heart of a child; but the rod of correction shall drive it far from him.

23:13-14 Withhold not correction from the child: for if thou beatest him with the rod, he shall not die. Thou shalt beat him with the rod, and shalt deliver his soul from hell.

23:24-25 The father of the righteous shall greatly rejoice: and he that begetteth a wise child shall have joy of him. Thy father and thy mother shall be glad, and she that bare thee shall rejoice.

29:15 The rod and reproof give wisdom: but a child left to himself bringeth his mother to shame.

29:17 Correct thy son, and he shall give thee rest; yea, he shall give delight unto thy soul.

## *PEACE*

3:24 When thou liest down, thou shalt not be afraid: yea, thou shalt lie down, and thy sleep shall be sweet.

3:30 Strive not with a man without cause, if he have done thee no harm.

3:2 For length of days, and long life, and peace, shall they add to thee.

12:20 Deceit is in the heart of them that imagine evil: but to the counsellors of peace is joy.

16:7 When a man's ways please the LORD, he maketh even his enemies to be at peace with him.

17:1 Better is a dry morsel, and quietness therewith, than an house full of sacrifices with strife.

20:3 It is an honour for a man to cease from strife: but every fool will be meddling.

24:19 Fret not thyself because of evil men, neither be thou envious at the wicked;

## *PERVERSENESS* - (WAYWARD)

11:3 The integrity of the upright shall guide them: but the perverseness of transgressors shall destroy them.

12:8 A man shall be commended according to his wisdom: but he that is of a perverse heart shall be despised.

14:2 He that walketh in his uprightness feareth the LORD: but he that is perverse in his ways despiseth him.

17:20 He that hath a froward heart findeth no good: and he that hath a perverse tongue falleth into mischief.

28:6 Better is the poor that walketh in his uprightness, than he that is perverse in his ways, though he be rich.

28:18 Whoso walketh uprightly shall be saved: but he that is perverse in his ways shall fall at once.

## *The POOR*

14:20 The poor is hated even of his own neighbour: but the rich hath many friends.

14:31 He that oppresseth the poor reproacheth his Maker: but he that honoureth him hath mercy on the poor

17:5 Whoso mocketh the poor reproacheth his Maker: and he that is glad at calamities shall not be unpunished.

18:23 The poor useth entreaties; but the rich answereth roughly.

19:1 Better is the poor that walketh in his integrity, than he that is perverse in his lips, and is a fool.

19:4 Wealth maketh many friends; but the poor is separated from his neighbour.

19:7 All the brethren of the poor do hate him: how much more do his friends go far from him? he pursueth them with words, yet they are wanting to him.

20:13 Love not sleep, lest thou come to poverty; open thine eyes, and thou shalt be satisfied with bread.

21:17 He that loveth pleasure shall be a poor man: he that loveth wine and oil shall not be rich.

22:2 The rich and poor meet together: the LORD is the maker of them all.

22:22 Rob not the poor, because he is poor: neither oppress the afflicted in the gate:

23:21 For the drunkard and the glutton shall come to poverty: and drowsiness shall clothe a man with rags.

28:6 Better is the poor that walketh in his uprightness, than he that is perverse in his ways, though he be rich.

10:4 He becometh poor that dealeth with a slack hand: but the hand of the diligent maketh rich.

19:22 The desire of a man is his kindness: and a man is better than a liar.

## *PRAYER*

1:28-29 Then shall they call upon me, but I will not answer; they shall seek me early, but they shall not find me: For that they hated knowledge, and did not choose the fear of the LORD:

15:8 The sacrifice of the wicked is an abomination to the LORD: but the prayer of the upright is his delight.

15:29 The LORD is far from the wicked: but he heareth the prayer of the righteous.

28:9 He that turneth away his ear from hearing the law, even his prayer shall be abomination.

## *PRIDE*

3:7 Be not wise in thine own eyes: fear the LORD, and depart from evil.

8:13 The fear of the LORD is to hate evil: pride, and arrogancy, and the evil way, and the froward mouth, do I hate.

11:2 When pride cometh, then cometh shame: but with the lowly is wisdom.

13:10 Only by pride cometh contention: but with the well advised is wisdom.

14:3 In the mouth of the foolish is a rod of pride: but the lips of the wise shall preserve them.

15:25 The LORD will destroy the house of the proud: but he will establish the border of the widow.

16:2 All the ways of a man are clean in his own eyes; but the LORD weigheth the spirits.

16:5 Every one that is proud in heart is an abomination to the LORD: though hand join in hand, he shall not be unpunished.

16:18 Pride goeth before destruction, and an haughty spirit before a fall.

18:11 The rich man's wealth is his strong city, and as an high wall in his own conceit.

20:6 Most men will proclaim every one his own goodness: but a faithful man who can find?

21:2 Every way of a man is right in his own eyes: but the LORD pondereth the hearts.

21:4 An high look, and a proud heart, and the plowing of the wicked, is sin.

25:6-7 Put not forth thyself in the presence of the king, and stand not in the place of great men: For better it is that it be said unto thee, Come up hither; than that thou shouldest be put lower in the presence of the prince whom thine eyes have seen.

25:14 Whoso boasteth himself of a false gift is like clouds and wind without rain.

25:27 It is not good to eat much honey: so for men to search their own glory is not glory.

26:12 Seest thou a man wise in his own conceit? there is more hope of a fool than of him.

28:25 He that is of a proud heart stirreth up strife: but he that putteth his trust in the LORD shall be made fat.

29:23 A man's pride shall bring him low: but honour shall uphold the humble in spirit.

30:13 There is a generation, O how lofty are their eyes! and their eyelids are lifted up.

## *PRUDENCE*

8:12 I wisdom dwell with prudence, and find out knowledge of witty inventions.

12:16 A fool's wrath is presently known: but a prudent man covereth shame.

12:23 A prudent man concealeth knowledge: but the heart of fools proclaimeth foolishness.

13:16 Every prudent man dealeth with knowledge: but a fool layeth open his folly.

14:8 The wisdom of the prudent is to understand his way: but the folly of fools is deceit.

14:15 The simple believeth every word: but the prudent man looketh well to his going.

14:18 The simple inherit folly: but the prudent are crowned with knowledge.

15:5 A fool despiseth his father's instruction: but he that regardeth reproof is prudent.

16:21 The wise in heart shall be called prudent: and the sweetness of the lips increaseth learning.

22:3 A prudent man foreseeth the evil, and hideth himself: but the simple pass on, and are punished.

## *REBELLION*

1:24 Because I have called, and ye refused; I have stretched out my hand, and no man regarded;

5:12 And say, How have I hated instruction, and my heart despised reproof;

17:11 An evil man seeketh only rebellion: therefore a cruel messenger shall be sent against him.

19:28 An ungodly witness scorneth judgment: and the mouth of the wicked devoureth iniquity.

## *REPROOF*

1:23 Turn you at my reproof: behold, I will pour out my spirit unto you, I will make known my words unto you.

1:25 But ye have set at nought all my counsel, and would none of my reproof:

1:30 They would none of my counsel: they despised all my reproof.

5:12 And say, How have I hated instruction, and my heart despised reproof;

6:23 For the commandment is a lamp; and the law is light; and reproofs of instruction are the way of life:

9:7-8 He that reproveth a scorner getteth to himself shame: and he that rebuketh a wicked man getteth himself a blot. Reprove not a scorner, lest he hate thee: rebuke a wise man, and he will love thee.

10:17 He is in the way of life that keepeth instruction: but he that refuseth reproof erreth.

12:1 Whoso loveth instruction loveth knowledge: but he that hateth reproof is brutish.

13:1 A wise son heareth his father's instruction: but a scorner heareth not rebuke.

13:18 Poverty and shame shall be to him that refuseth instruction: but he that regardeth reproof shall be honoured.

15:5 A fool despiseth his father's instruction: but he that regardeth reproof is prudent.

15:10 Correction is grievous unto him that forsaketh the way: and he that hateth reproof shall die.

15:12 A scorner loveth not one that reproveth him: neither will he go unto the wise.

15:32 He that refuseth instruction despiseth his own soul: but he that heareth reproof getteth understanding.

17:10 A reproof entereth more into a wise man than an hundred stripes into a fool.

19:25 Smite a scorner, and the simple will beware: and reprove one that hath understanding, and he will understand knowledge.

27:5 Open rebuke is better than secret love.

28:23 He that rebuketh a man afterwards shall find more favour than he that flattereth with the tongue.

29:1 He, that being often reproved hardeneth his neck, shall suddenly be destroyed, and that without remedy.

29:15 The rod and reproof give wisdom: but a child left to himself bringeth his mother to shame.

## *REWARDS*

3:10 So shall thy barns be filled with plenty, and thy presses shall burst out with new wine.

8:21 That I may cause those that love me to inherit substance; and I will fill their treasures.

11:18 The wicked worketh a deceitful work: but to him that soweth righteousness shall be a sure reward.

11:25 The liberal soul shall be made fat: and he that watereth shall be watered also himself.

11:28 He that trusteth in his riches shall fall: but the righteous shall flourish as a branch.

11:29 He that troubleth his own house shall inherit the wind: and the fool shall be servant to the wise of heart.

11:30 The fruit of the righteous is a tree of life; and he that winneth souls is wise.

12:2 A good man obtaineth favour of the LORD: but a man of wicked devices will he condemn.

13:13 Whoso despiseth the word shall be destroyed: but he that feareth the commandment shall be rewarded.

17:13 Whoso rewardeth evil for good, evil shall not depart from his house.

26:10 The great God that formed all things both rewardeth the fool, and rewardeth transgressors.

## **RIGHTEOUSNESS**

2:7 He layeth up sound wisdom for the righteous: he is a buckler to them that walk uprightly.

4:18 But the path of the just is as the shining light, that shineth more and more unto the perfect day.

10:2-3 Treasures of wickedness profit nothing: but righteousness delivereth from death. The LORD will not suffer the soul of the righteous to famish: but he casteth away the substance of the wicked.

10:21 The lips of the righteous feed many: but fools die for want of wisdom.

10:24 The fear of the wicked, it shall come upon him: but the desire of the righteous shall be granted.

10:30 The righteous shall never be removed: but the wicked shall not inhabit the earth.

11:4-6 Riches profit not in the day of wrath: but righteousness delivereth from death. The righteousness of the perfect shall direct his way: but the wicked shall fall by his own wickedness. The righteousness of the upright shall deliver them: but transgressors shall be taken in their own naughtiness.

11:8 The righteous is delivered out of trouble, and the wicked cometh in his stead.

11:11 By the blessing of the upright the city is exalted: but it is overthrown by the mouth of the wicked.

11:19 As righteousness tendeth to life: so he that pursueth evil pursueth it to his own death.

11:23 The desire of the righteous is only good: but the expectation of the wicked is wrath.

11:28 He that trusteth in his riches shall fall: but the righteous shall flourish as a branch.

11:30 The fruit of the righteous is a tree of life; and he that winneth souls is wise.

12:5 The thoughts of the righteous are right: but the counsels of the wicked are deceit.

12:7 The wicked are overthrown, and are not: but the house of the righteous shall stand.

12:28 In the way of righteousness is life; and in the pathway thereof there is no death.

13:6 Righteousness keepeth him that is upright in the way: but wickedness overthroweth the sinner.

13:9 The light of the righteous rejoiceth: but the lamp of the wicked shall be put out.

14:34 Righteousness exalteth a nation: but sin is a reproach to any people.

21:12 The righteous man wisely considereth the house of the wicked: but God overthroweth the wicked for their wickedness.

21:21 He that followeth after righteousness and mercy findeth life, righteousness, and honour.

28:1 The wicked flee when no man pursueth: but the righteous are bold as a lion.

28:1 The wicked flee when no man pursueth: but the righteous are bold as a lion.

29:2 When the righteous are in authority, the people rejoice: but when the wicked beareth rule, the people mourn.

29:6-7 In the transgression of an evil man there is a snare: but the righteous doth sing and rejoice. The righteous considereth the cause of the poor: but the wicked regardeth not to know it.

## *SALVATION*

8:35 For whoso findeth me findeth life, and shall obtain favour of the LORD.

20:22 Say not thou, I will recompense evil; but wait on the LORD, and he shall save thee.

28:18 Whoso walketh uprightly shall be saved: but he that is perverse in his ways shall fall at once.

**FIVE THINGS GOD WANTS YOU TO KNOW ABOUT SALVATION.**

### *I. You need to be saved.*

Romans 3:10 As it is written, There is none righteous, no, not one:

Romans 3:23 For all have sinned, and come short of the glory of God;

> Note: If you would die in your natural condition you would be separated from God and go to hell.

## *II. You cannot save yourself.*

Ephesians 2:8-9 For by grace are ye saved through faith; and that not of yourselves: it is the gift of God: Not of works, lest any man should boast.

Titus 3:5 Not by works of righteousness which we have done, but according to his mercy he saved us, by the washing of regeneration, and renewing of the Holy Ghost;

## *III. Jesus has provided your salvation.*

John 3:16 For God so loved the world, that he gave his only begotten Son, that whosoever believeth in him should not perish, but have everlasting life.

John 14:6 Jesus saith unto him, I am the way, the truth, and the life: no man cometh unto the Father, but by me.

Acts 4:12 Neither is there salvation in any other: for there is none other name under heaven given among men, whereby we must be saved.

## *IV. You must accept Jesus for salvation.*

Acts 16:31 And they said, Believe on the Lord Jesus Christ, and thou shalt be saved, and thy house.

John 1:12 But as many as received him, to them gave he power to become the sons of God, even to them that believe on his name:

Revelation 3:20 Behold, I stand at the door, and knock: if any man hear my voice, and open the door, I will come in to him, and will sup with him, and he with me.

## ***V. Now is the time to accept Jesus Christ as your Savior.***

2 Corinthians 6:2 (For he saith, I have heard thee in a time accepted, and in the day of salvation have I succoured thee: behold, now is the accepted time; behold, now is the day of salvation.)

**Dear Reader**, If you would like to receive Christ as your Savior, simply pray this prayer from your heart:

Dear Lord Jesus, I confess that I am a sinner. Please forgive me of all my sins. I believe you are the only Saviour, and that you died for my sins, and was buried and three days you arose physically from the grave never to die again. I ask You to come into my heart right now and save me. Thank You Lord Jesus for coming in to my heart as You promised. In Jesus Name I pray, Amen.

Dear Friend, If you have prayed to receive Christ as your Savior, please write me (bama4u@bellsouth.net) and tell me about it. Please copy this link into your internet browser and view the videos at www.bama4u.org/heaven2.htm.

For an interesting video please download this QR Code on your Smartphone and scan this code for a 12 minutet video presentation that could change your life forever. May God bless you.

## *SCORN*

1:22 How long, ye simple ones, will ye love simplicity? and the scorners delight in their scorning, and fools hate knowledge?

3:34 Surely he scorneth the scorners: but he giveth grace unto the lowly.

9:7-8 He that reproveth a scorner getteth to himself shame: and he that rebuketh a wicked man getteth himself a blot. Reprove not a scorner, lest he hate thee: rebuke a wise man, and he will love thee.

9:12 If thou be wise, thou shalt be wise for thyself: but if thou scornest, thou alone shalt bear it.

13:1 A wise son heareth his father's instruction: but a scorner heareth not rebuke.

14:6 A scorner seeketh wisdom, and findeth it not: but knowledge is easy unto him that understandeth.

15:12 A scorner loveth not one that reproveth him: neither will he go unto the wise.

19:29 Judgments are prepared for scorners, and stripes for the back of fools.

22:10 Cast out the scorner, and contention shall go out; yea, strife and reproach shall cease.

24:9 The thought of foolishness is sin: and the scorner is an abomination to men.

29:8 Scornful men bring a city into a snare: but wise men turn away wrath.

## *SELF CONTROL*

4:23 Keep thy heart with all diligence; for out of it are the issues of life.

16:33 The lot is cast into the lap; but the whole disposing thereof is of the LORD.

21:2 Every way of a man is right in his own eyes: but the LORD pondereth the hearts.

25:15 By long forbearing is a prince persuaded, and a soft tongue breaketh the bone.

25:28 He that hath no rule over his own spirit is like a city that is broken down, and without walls.

## *SELF-WILL*

1:24 Because I have called, and ye refused; I have stretched out my hand, and no man regarded;

1:31 Therefore shall they eat of the fruit of their own way, and be filled with their own devices.

3:5 Trust in the LORD with all thine heart; and lean not unto thine own understanding.

3:7 Be not wise in thine own eyes: fear the LORD, and depart from evil.

14:12 There is a way which seemeth right unto a man, but the end thereof are the ways of death.

14:14 The backslider in heart shall be filled with his own ways: and a good man shall be satisfied from himself.

15:32 He that refuseth instruction despiseth his own soul: but he that heareth reproof getteth understanding.

16:2 All the ways of a man are clean in his own eyes; but the LORD weigheth the spirits.

20:24 Man's goings are of the LORD; how can a man then understand his own way?

21:2 Every way of a man is right in his own eyes: but the LORD pondereth the hearts.

25:28 He that hath no rule over his own spirit is like a city that is broken down, and without walls.

28:26 He that trusteth in his own heart is a fool: but whoso walketh wisely, he shall be delivered.

29:1 He, that being often reproved hardeneth his neck, shall suddenly be destroyed, and that without remedy.

30:12 There is a generation that are pure in their own eyes, and yet is not washed from their filthiness.

## *SEXUAL IMPURITY*

2:16-19 To deliver thee from the strange woman, even from the stranger which flattereth with her words; Which forsaketh the guide of her youth, and forgetteth the covenant of her God. For her house inclineth unto death, and her paths unto the dead. None that go unto her return again, neither take they hold of the paths of life.

5:3-5 For the lips of a strange woman drop as an honeycomb, and her mouth is smoother than oil: But her end is bitter as wormwood, sharp as a twoedged sword. Her feet go down to death; her steps take hold on hell.

5:20 And why wilt thou, my son, be ravished with a strange woman, and embrace the bosom of a stranger?

**6:24-29** For the commandment is a lamp; and the law is light; and reproofs of instruction are the way of life: To keep thee from the evil woman, from the flattery of the tongue of a strange woman. Lust not after her beauty in thine heart; neither let her take thee with her eyelids. For by means of a whorish woman a man is brought to a piece of bread: and the adulteress will hunt for the precious life. Can a man take fire in his bosom, and his clothes not be burned? Can one go upon hot coals, and his feet not be burned? So he that goeth in to his neighbour's wife; whosoever toucheth her shall not be innocent.

6:32 But whoso committeth adultery with a woman lacketh understanding: he that doeth it destroyeth his own soul.

7:6-27 For at the window of my house I looked through my casement, And beheld among the simple ones, I discerned among the youths, a young man void of understanding, Passing through the street near her corner; and he went the way to her house, In the twilight, in the evening, in the black and dark night: And, behold, there met him a woman with the attire of an harlot, and subtil of heart. (She is loud and stubborn; her feet abide not in her house: Now is she without, now in the streets, and lieth in wait at every corner.) So she caught him, and kissed him, and with have peace offerings with me; this day have I payed my vows. Therefore came I forth to meet thee, diligently to seek thy face, and I have found thee. I have decked my bed with coverings of tapestry, with carved works, with fine linen of Egypt. I have perfumed my bed with Come, let us take our fill of love until the morning: let us solace ourselves with loves. For the goodman is not at home, he is gone a long journey: He hath taken a bag of money with him, and will come home at the day appointed. With her much fair speech she caused him to yield, with the flattering of her lips she forced him. He goeth after her straightway, as an ox goeth to the slaughter, or as a fool to the correction of the stocks; Till a dart strike through his liver; as a bird hasteth to the snare, and knoweth not that it is for his life. Hearken unto me now therefore, O ye children, and attend to the words of my mouth. Let not thine heart decline to her ways, go not astray in her paths. For she hath cast down many wounded: yea, many strong men have been slain by her. Her house is the way to hell, going down to the chambers of death.

22:14 The mouth of strange women is a deep pit: he that is abhorred of the LORD shall fall therein.

23:27-28 For a whore is a deep ditch; and a strange woman is a narrow pit. She also lieth in wait as for a prey, and increaseth the transgressors among men.

29:3 Whoso loveth wisdom rejoiceth his father: but he that keepeth company with harlots spendeth his substance.

30:20 Such is the way of an adulterous woman; she eateth, and wipeth her mouth, and saith, I have done no wickedness.

31:3 Give not thy strength unto women, nor thy ways to that which destroyeth kings.

## *SIN*

1:10 My son, if sinners entice thee, consent thou not.

8:36 But he that sinneth against me wrongeth his own soul: all they that hate me love death.

10:16 The labour of the righteous tendeth to life: the fruit of the wicked to sin.

13:6 Righteousness keepeth him that is upright in the way: but wickedness overthroweth the sinner.

13:21 Evil pursueth sinners: but to the righteous good shall be repayed.

13:22 A good man leaveth an inheritance to his children's children: and the wealth of the sinner is laid up for the just.

14:9 Fools make a mock at sin: but among the righteous there is favour.

14:14 The backslider in heart shall be filled with his own ways: and a good man shall be satisfied from himself.

14:21 He that despiseth his neighbour sinneth: but he that hath mercy on the poor, happy is he.

14:34 Righteousness exalteth a nation: but sin is a reproach to any people.

20:9 Who can say, I have made my heart clean, I am pure from my sin?

21:4 An high look, and a proud heart, and the plowing of the wicked, is sin.

21:15 It is joy to the just to do judgment: but destruction shall be to the workers of iniquity.

23:17 Let not thine heart envy sinners: but be thou in the fear of the LORD all the day long.

24:9 The thought of foolishness is sin: and the scorner is an abomination to men.

28:13 He that covereth his sins shall not prosper: but whoso confesseth and forsaketh them shall have mercy.

## *SOUL WINNING*

11:30 The fruit of the righteous is a tree of life; and he that winneth souls is wise.

14:5 A faithful witness will not lie: but a false witness will utter lies.

14:25 A true witness delivereth souls: but a deceitful witness speaketh lies.

> For more information on how to become an effective soul winner, please copy this link into your internet browser:
> http://bama4u.org/EVANGELISM/0.%20SOUL%20WINNING.htm

## *STEALING*

9:17 Stolen waters are sweet, and bread eaten in secret is pleasant.

11:1 A false balance is abomination to the LORD: but a just weight is his delight.

21:7 The robbery of the wicked shall destroy them; because they refuse to do judgment.

28:24 Whoso robbeth his father or his mother, and saith, It is no transgression; the same is the companion of a destroyer.

29:24 Whoso is partner with a thief hateth his own soul: he heareth cursing, and bewrayeth it not.

## *STRIFE*

3:30 Strive not with a man without cause, if he have done thee no harm.

10:12 Hatred stirreth up strifes: but love covereth all sins.

11:29 He that troubleth his own house shall inherit the wind: and the fool shall be servant to the wise of heart.

13:10 Only by pride cometh contention: but with the well advised is wisdom.

15:18 A wrathful man stirreth up strife: but he that is slow to anger appeaseth strife.

16:28 A froward man soweth strife: and a whisperer separateth chief friends.

17:1 Better is a dry morsel, and quietness therewith, than an house full of sacrifices with strife.

17:14 The beginning of strife is as when one letteth out water: therefore leave off contention, before it be meddled with.

17:19 He loveth transgression that loveth strife: and he that exalteth his gate seeketh destruction.

20:3 It is an honour for a man to cease from strife: but every fool will be meddling.

22:10 Cast out the scorner, and contention shall go out; yea, strife and reproach shall cease.26:17 He that passeth by, and meddleth with strife belonging not to him, is like one that taketh a dog by the ears.

26:21 As coals are to burning coals, and wood to fire; so is a contentious man to kindle strife.

## *TRUST*

3:5-6 Trust in the LORD with all thine heart; and lean not unto thine own understanding. In all thy ways acknowledge him, and he shall direct thy paths.

11:28 He that trusteth in his riches shall fall: but the righteous shall flourish as a branch.

16:3 Commit thy works unto the LORD, and thy thoughts shall be established.

16:20 He that handleth a matter wisely shall find good: and whoso trusteth in the LORD, happy is he.

20:22 Say not thou, I will recompense evil; but wait on the LORD, and he shall save thee.

22:19 That thy trust may be in the LORD, I have made known to thee this day, even to thee.

24:10 If thou faint in the day of adversity, thy strength is small.

28:5 Evil men understand not judgment: but they that seek the LORD understand all things.

28:25 He that is of a proud heart stirreth up strife: but he that putteth his trust in the LORD shall be made fat.

28:26 He that trusteth in his own heart is a fool: but whoso walketh wisely, he shall be delivered.

29:25 The fear of man bringeth a snare: but whoso putteth his trust in the LORD shall be safe.

30:5 Every word of God is pure: he is a shield unto them that put their trust in him.

## *TRUTH*

3:3 Let not mercy and truth forsake thee: bind them about thy neck; write them upon the table of thine heart:

12:17 He that speaketh truth sheweth forth righteousness: but a false witness deceit.

12:19 The lip of truth shall be established for ever: but a lying tongue is but for a moment.

12:22 Lying lips are abomination to the LORD: but they that deal truly are his delight.

14:22 Do they not err that devise evil? but mercy and truth shall be to them that devise good.

16:6 By mercy and truth iniquity is purged: and by the fear of the LORD men depart from evil.

23:23 Buy the truth, and sell it not; also wisdom, and instruction, and understanding.

## *UNDERSTANDING*

1:5 A wise man will hear, and will increase learning; and a man of understanding shall attain unto wise counsels:

2:11 Discretion shall preserve thee, understanding shall keep thee:

3:13 Happy is the man that findeth wisdom, and the man that getteth understanding.

4:1 Hear, ye children, the instruction of a father, and attend to know understanding.

4:5 Get wisdom, get understanding: forget it not; neither decline from the words of my mouth.

4:7 Wisdom is the principal thing; therefore get wisdom: and with all thy getting get understanding.

5:1 My son, attend unto my wisdom, and bow thine ear to my understanding:

7:4 Say unto wisdom, Thou art my sister; and call understanding thy kinswoman:

9:6 Forsake the foolish, and live; and go in the way of understanding.

10:13 In the lips of him that hath understanding wisdom is found: but a rod is for the back of him that is void of understanding.

10:23 It is as sport to a fool to do mischief: but a man of understanding hath wisdom.

11:12 He that is void of wisdom despiseth his neighbour: but a man of understanding holdeth his peace.

15:14 The heart of him that hath understanding seeketh knowledge: but the mouth of fools feedeth on foolishness.

15:21 Folly is joy to him that is destitute of wisdom: but a man of understanding walketh uprightly.

16:22 Understanding is a wellspring of life unto him that hath it: but the instruction of fools is folly.

19:8 He that getteth wisdom loveth his own soul: he that keepeth understanding shall find good.

24:3 Through wisdom is an house builded; and by understanding it is established:

28:5 Evil men understand not judgment: but they that seek the LORD understand all things.

## *WEALTH*

11:4 Riches profit not in the day of wrath: but righteousness delivereth from death.

11:28 He that trusteth in his riches shall fall: but the righteous shall flourish as a branch.

13:8 The ransom of a man's life are his riches: but the poor heareth not rebuke.

13:11 Wealth gotten by vanity shall be diminished: but he that gathereth by labour shall increase.

13:22 A good man leaveth an inheritance to his children's children: and the wealth of the sinner is laid up for the just.

14:20 The poor is hated even of his own neighbour: but the rich hath many friends.

18:11 The rich man's wealth is his strong city, and as an high wall in his own conceit.

18:23 The poor useth entreaties; but the rich answereth roughly.

19:4 Wealth maketh many friends; but the poor is separated from his neighbour.

19:6 Many will entreat the favour of the prince: and every man is a friend to him that giveth gifts.

22:2 The rich and poor meet together: the LORD is the maker of them all.

22:7 The rich ruleth over the poor, and the borrower is servant to the lender.

23:4 Labour not to be rich: cease from thine own wisdom.

27:24 For riches are not for ever: and doth the crown endure to every generation? conceit; but the poor that hath understanding searcheth him out.

28:11 The rich man is wise in his own conceit; but the poor that hath understanding searcheth him out.

28:20 A faithful man shall abound with blessings: but he that maketh haste to be rich shall not be innocent.

28:22 He that hasteth to be rich hath an evil eye, and considereth not that poverty shall come upon him.

## *WICKED*

2:22 But the wicked shall be cut off from the earth, and the transgressors shall be rooted out of it.

3:33 The curse of the LORD is in the house of the wicked: but he blesseth the habitation of the just.

4:14 Enter not into the path of the wicked, and go not in the way of evil men.

4:19 The way of the wicked is as darkness: they know not at what they stumble.

5:22 His own iniquities shall take the wicked himself, and he shall be holden with the cords of his sins.

6:12 A naughty person, a wicked man, walketh with a froward mouth.

10:2-3 Treasures of wickedness profit nothing: but righteousness delivereth from death. The LORD will not suffer the soul of the righteous to famish: but he casteth away the substance of the wicked.

10:6-7 Blessings are upon the head of the just: but violence covereth the mouth of the wicked. The memory of the just is blessed: but the name of the wicked shall rot.

10:30 The righteous shall never be removed: but the wicked shall not inhabit the earth.

11:5 The righteousness of the perfect shall direct his way: but the wicked shall fall by his own wickedness.

11:7 When a wicked man dieth, his expectation shall perish: and the hope of unjust men perisheth.

11:10 When it goeth well with the righteous, the city rejoiceth: and when the wicked perish, there is shouting.

11:18 The wicked worketh a deceitful work: but to him that soweth righteousness shall be a sure reward.

11:21 Though hand join in hand, the wicked shall not be unpunished: but the seed of the righteous shall be delivered.

12:5 The thoughts of the righteous are right: but the counsels of the wicked are deceit.

12:7 The wicked are overthrown, and are not: but the house of the righteous shall stand.

12:13 The wicked is snared by the transgression of his lips: but the just shall come out of trouble.

13:9 The light of the righteous rejoiceth: but the lamp of the wicked shall be put out.

14:11 The house of the wicked shall be overthrown: but the tabernacle of the upright shall flourish.

18:3 When the wicked cometh, then cometh also contempt, and with ignominy reproach.

21:10 The soul of the wicked desireth evil: his neighbour findeth no favour in his eyes.

21:29 A wicked man hardeneth his face: but as for the upright, he directeth his way.

24:16 For a just man falleth seven times, and riseth up again: but the wicked shall fall into mischief.

28:1 The wicked flee when no man pursueth: but the righteous are bold as a lion.

29:2 When the righteous are in authority, the people rejoice: but when the wicked beareth rule, the people mourn.

# *WISDOM* (Knowledge applied correctly)

1:5 A wise man will hear, and will increase learning; and a man of understanding shall attain unto wise counsels:

2:6 For the LORD giveth wisdom: out of his mouth cometh knowledge and understanding.

3:13 Happy is the man that findeth wisdom, and the man that getteth understanding.

3:35 The wise shall inherit glory: but shame shall be the promotion of fools.

4:5 Get wisdom, get understanding: forget it not; neither decline from the words of my mouth.

4:7 Wisdom is the principal thing; therefore get wisdom: and with all thy getting get understanding.

5:1 My son, attend unto my wisdom, and bow thine ear to my understanding:

7:4 Say unto wisdom, Thou art my sister; and call understanding thy kinswoman:

8:11 For wisdom is better than rubies; and all the things that may be desired are not to be compared to it.

9:10 The fear of the LORD is the beginning of wisdom: and the knowledge of the holy is understanding.

10:14 Wise men lay up knowledge: but the mouth of the foolish is near destruction.

13:20 He that walketh with wise men shall be wise: but a companion of fools shall be destroyed.

14:3 In the mouth of the foolish is a rod of pride: but the lips of the wise shall preserve them.

14:16 A wise man feareth, and departeth from evil: but the fool rageth, and is confident.

16:16 How much better is it to get wisdom than gold! and to get understanding rather to be chosen than silver!

19:8 He that getteth wisdom loveth his own soul: he that keepeth understanding shall find good.

21:11 When the scorner is punished, the simple is made wise: and when the wise is instructed, he receiveth knowledge.

21:22 A wise man scaleth the city of the mighty, and casteth down the strength of the confidence thereof.

24:3 Through wisdom is an house builded; and by understanding it is established:

29:3 Whoso loveth wisdom rejoiceth his father: but he that keepeth company with harlots spendeth his substance.

## *WIVES*

5:18-19 Let thy fountain be blessed: and rejoice with the wife of thy youth. Let her be as the loving hind and pleasant roe; let her breasts satisfy thee at all times; and be thou ravished always with her love.

12:4 A virtuous woman is a crown to her husband: but she that maketh ashamed is as rottenness in his bones.

14:1 Every wise woman buildeth her house: but the foolish plucketh it down with her hands.

18:22 Whoso findeth a wife findeth a good thing, and obtaineth favour of the LORD.

19:13 A foolish son is the calamity of his father: and the contentions of a wife are a continual dropping.

19:14 House and riches are the inheritance of fathers: and a prudent wife is from the LORD.

21:19 It is better to dwell in the wilderness, than with a contentious and an angry woman.

25:24 It is better to dwell in the corner of the housetop, than with a brawling woman and in a wide house.

27:15 A continual dropping in a very rainy day and a contentious woman are alike.

31:10-31 Who can find a virtuous woman? for her price is far above rubies. The heart of her husband doth safely trust in her, so that he shall have no need of spoil. She will do him good and not evil all the days of her life. She seeketh wool, and flax, and worketh willingly with her hands. She is like the merchants' ships; she bringeth her food from afar. She riseth also while it is yet night, and giveth meat to her household, and a portion to her maidens. She considereth a field, and buyeth it: with the fruit of her hands she planteth a vineyard. She girdeth her loins with strength, and strengtheneth her arms. She perceiveth that her merchandise is good: her candle goeth not out by night. She layeth her hands to the spindle, and her hands hold the distaff. She stretcheth out her hand to the poor; yea, she reacheth forth her hands to the needy. She is not afraid of the snow for her household: for all her household are clothed with scarlet. She maketh herself coverings of tapestry; her clothing is silk and purple. Her husband is known in the gates, when he sitteth among the elders of the land. She maketh fine linen, and selleth it; and delivereth girdles unto the merchant. Strength and honour are her clothing; and she shall rejoice in time to come. She openeth her mouth with wisdom; and in her tongue is the law of kindness. She looketh well to the ways of her household, and eateth not the bread of idleness. Her children arise up, and call her blessed; her husband also, and he praiseth her. Many daughters have done virtuously, but thou excellest them all. Favour is deceitful, and beauty is vain: but a woman that feareth Give her of the fruit of her hands; and let her own works praise her in the gates.

# *WOMEN*

2:16-17 To deliver thee from the strange woman, even from the stranger which flattereth with her words; Which forsaketh the guide of her youth, and forgetteth the covenant of her God.

9:13 A foolish woman is clamorous: she is simple, and knoweth nothing.

11:16 A gracious woman retaineth honour: and strong men retain riches.

11:22 As a jewel of gold in a swine's snout, so is a fair woman which is without discretion.

27:15 A continual dropping in a very rainy day and a contentious woman are alike.

31:10 Who can find a virtuous woman? for her price is far above rubies.

Please check out these interesting, helpful, and easy to read books by Mel Brown on Amazon.com

Mickey Park says: *"But we have this treasure in earthen vessels, that the excellency of the power may be of God and not of us."* Mel Brown - his family background, his personal, practical interest and skills, his passion for souls, his sense of understanding of how to bring the Gospel to a different culture and God using that man is 2 Cor. 4:7 in living color. Mel overcame personal challenges, survived rough spots in his ministry journey, but in it all never lost His heart for God or his desire to see people brought to salvation.

From my experience with hundreds of servants of God on foreign fields, Mel and his gifted helpmeet, Carol, were uniquely used of God to build a self sustaining indigenous ministry rarely seen. When you read the story you will "Amen" 2 Corinthians 4:7."
**Rev. Mickey Park**, Pastor and Missionary

# "HOW TO GET MORE MONEY FROM GOD"

which will be available early 2017 on Amazon.com. This book will teach you and your church how to become self supporting. It is a proven technique based on the promises of God.

This is the book our graduates taught their new converts / churches what the Bible says about stewardship. Their members were blessed and prospered by this series. The results cannot lie. It really works!

Made in the USA
Columbia, SC
24 July 2023